Cath Senker | **How to get ahead in**

Construction

www.raintreepublishers.co.uk

Visit our website to find out more information about **Raintree** books.

To order:

☎ Phone 44 (0) 1865 888113

🖹 Send a fax to 44 (0) 1865 314091

💻 Visit the Raintree bookshop at **www.raintreepublishers.co.uk** to browse our catalogue and order online.

First published in Great Britain by Raintree, Halley Court, Jordan Hill, Oxford OX2 8EJ, part of Harcourt Education.
Raintree is a registered trademark of Harcourt Education Ltd.

© Harcourt Education Ltd 2007
The moral right of the proprietor has been asserted.

Editorial: Melanie Waldron and Lucy Beevor
Design: David Poole and Calcium
Illustrations: Geoff Ward
Picture Research: Melissa Allison and Fiona Orbell
Production: Huseyin Sami

Originated by Chroma Graphics
Printed and bound in China by South China Printing Company

10 digit ISBN 1 406 20440 4
13 digit ISBN 978 1 406 20440 7

11 10 09 08 07
10 9 8 7 6 5 4 3 2 1

British Library Cataloguing in Publication Data
Senker, Cath
Construction. – (How to get ahead in)
624.'02341
A full catalogue record for this book is available from the British Library.

Acknowledgements
The publishers would like to thank the following for permission to reproduce photographs: Alamy pp. 14 (Bill Bachmann), 19 (David Hoffman Photo Library), 24 (Frances Roberts), 39 (Jeff Morgan), 18 (Norma Joseph), 23 (Photofusion Picture Library), 15 (Stock Connection Distribution); Corbis pp. 11 (Annie Griffiths Belt), 26 (MacDuff Everton), 7 (Paul A. Souders), 5 (Roger Ressmeyer), 10 (Royalty-Free), 42 (Tom Stewart), 44 (Viviane Moos), 36 (zefa/Dietrich Rose), 27 (zefa/M. Deutsch), 45 (zefa/Martin Meyer), 12 (zefa/Stock Photos/Lance Nelson); Edifice p. 17 (Sally Ann Norman); Education Photos p. 47 (Linda Westmore); Getty Images pp. 30 (DigitalVision), 21 (ImageBank), 37, 43 (Photodisc), 28 (Taxi); Liebherr Mining Equipment Co. p. 20 (Merilee Hunt); reportdigital.co.uk pp. 33 (John Harris), 35, 41 (Paul Box).

Cover photograph of building site reproduced with permission of TIPS Images/Marc Grimberg.

The author would like to thank the following for their help. Case studies: Daniel Hodge, David Brand, Sam Darlison, Mary Harrison, Liz Palfreman, Myrtle, Steve Thompson, Colin Vetters, Mike Wilding, and Andrew Woodward. Quotes: Holly Bennett (bconstructive); Catherine Harper (Learning and Skills Council); Paul Tudor (from Careers 2006, Trotman Publishing). Thanks also to Peter Senker for general information on the construction industry.

Contents

Words appearing in the text in bold, **like this**, are explained in the glossary.

So you think you might like to work in the construction industry? Well, you will find a huge variety of jobs out there.

Imagine what is needed to build a house. At first, old structures may need to be demolished. **Plant** operatives use heavy machinery to dig out the area so that the **foundations** can be laid. The exterior of the building is erected. Bricklayers build the walls and roofers construct the roof. Timber workers are needed because wood is essential in most structures. The interior **professionals** follow, fitting ceilings, laying floors, and tiling the walls and floors. Plumbers install the sanitary systems (sinks, baths, and toilets), draining systems, guttering, and central heating. Plasterers prepare the walls, ready for the painters and decorators to finish the job. As well as building jobs, there are many technical jobs associated with construction.

But the construction industry is not just about putting up buildings. You could be working on roads, bridges, car parks, or flood defences.

EXCITING PROJECTS

The Eden Project in Cornwall is an example of a recent large-scale construction project in the United Kingdom. There are three massive greenhouses, called biomes, which house different climate zones. The biomes span 100 metres without any inside supports!

Another exciting project is the Millennium Bridge in Gateshead – the world's first rotating bridge. It turns on pivots at both sides of the river to open and close – quite amazing.

CASE STUDY

Here, Liz – a civil engineer – describes her day.

*I'm a site engineer for a large **civil engineering** company. It is difficult to describe a typical day on site because I can honestly say that in 18 months of working on site no 2 days have been the same. This is one of the great things about site work – you never get bored. You can start the day planning to do one thing and end up doing a completely different thing because of unforeseen circumstances or bad weather.*

I usually start work at 7.30 a.m. I start by taking a walk around the site to check that everyone is there and knows what they will be working on that day. This is also a good opportunity to check that the site is safe and secure.

*My main responsibility is to make sure that no one is left standing with nothing to do. I have to make sure that all the **setting out** (transferring information from designer's drawings to the ground) is ready for work to begin. I also make sure that those who will be working on that section understand what is expected from them. After the work is complete, I then have to ensure that it has been finished correctly and to specification.*

below: *Construction projects can be enormous, involving many different people doing various jobs. This is the W. M. Keck Observatory under construction in Hawaii.*

Why work in construction?

Working in construction can bring great job satisfaction. As site engineer Liz says, 'I liked the idea of having something physical to show for my work – something that would be around for years that I could take my grandchildren to see and be able to say "I helped build that".'

Often, you will be building something that will make a big difference to people's lives. If you build flood defences near a village that has suffered in the past from flooding, you will be creating peace of mind for the local people. You might help to construct a bridge that will shorten people's journey to work and give them more leisure time.

Jobs galore

You can be sure to find a job in construction. Currently there are vacancies for about 86,000 people a year. There are many opportunities in the industry. You can work your way up from a low-level job and reach a supervisory or management position. Once you are qualified, there are opportunities to work abroad. You can also set up your own business and be your own boss. About 33 per cent of people in the UK construction industry are self-employed.

The construction industry can be exciting for young people because of sophisticated developments in techniques and equipment that require new skills. The government plans to build more prefabricated housing from ready-made parts, and workers need to be trained in specialist fixing and fitting skills. Increasing numbers of buildings include computers and advanced communication devices. If you're keen on IT at school, you will be in a good position to be trained for such work.

ECO-LIBRARY

The Jubilee Library in Brighton, Sussex, won an award in 2005 for its excellent construction, especially its sustainability. It draws most of its heat, light, and **ventilation** from the sun and sea breezes, has low energy consumption, and uses recycled rainwater. Find out how construction can be made more eco-friendly – start at www.ecoconstruction.org.

above: *The construction industry can involve working with new technology and practices all the time.*

Construction without destruction?

All building projects must comply with current environmental protection standards so you will be involved in this important aspect of the industry. The Government has a strategy for **sustainable** construction, so helping to conserve the environment should be part of your job. The aim is to:

◎ design for minimum waste
◎ produce less waste and pollution during construction
◎ use less energy in construction and use of the structure
◎ conserve water reserves
◎ respect the local environment.

Changing current practices towards sustainable alternatives presents an enormous challenge to the construction industry – are you up to the challenge?

CONSTRUCTION CAREER QUIZ

1   Where would you prefer to work?

   a) On site in the fresh air, whatever the weather

   b) In a nice, comfy office

2   Where do your talents lie?

   a) I like working with my hands, doing practical jobs

   b) I prefer planning and organizing tasks

3   Are you a technical person?

   a) Yes, I like to know how things work. I'd love to use different
      kinds of machinery and specialist tools.

   b) I would rather leave getting mucky to others

4   How fit and strong are you?

   a) I'm physically fit and could carry heavy equipment

   b) I'm a bit of a weakling

5   How would you cope with working in a difficult environment?

   a) I could cope with a bit of dust, dirt, and cold as long as I get
      a hot bath at the end of the day

   b) I'll stick to the nice, comfy office, thank you

6   Are you creative?

   a) I'm happy to leave the ideas to others. I'm more down-to-earth
      and practical.

   b) Yes, I'd like to put my creative ideas into practice

7 Would you be happy going to college full-time when you finish school?

a) No way! I'd like to start working and get my hands on some cash.

b) Yes, I'd rather be a student and get qualified before starting my career

8 What kind of employment situation would you prefer once you are trained?

a) I'd love to be my own boss and work independently

b) I'm a team worker. I'd like to be in charge of other people one day.

Quiz results

Choosing a career is not quite as simple as picking answers a) or b). But in general:

◎ If you answered a) more times than b), you might be interested in an on-site manual **trade** – see Chapters 1, 2, 3, and 7 for ideas. You can gain qualifications while working.

◎ If you answered mainly b), you may be keen on a desk job or starting your career at a higher level – see Chapters 4, 5, 7, and 8.

Whatever you think now, see if you can do some work experience to find out what the industry is really like – see Chapter 6.

WOMEN IN CONSTRUCTION

Construction is not just for men. About 10 per cent of construction workers are women. Find out what jobs women are doing in the industry by carrying out research on the Internet. Some useful websites are given in the Further information section on pages 50–53.

Chapter 1

Working with your hands

Do you have good hand-eye coordination? Can you cope with mathematical calculations? If you are good with your hands and at paying attention to detail, check out the trowel jobs and carpentry work. Or how about being an electrician?

Trowel work: get your hands in!

The trowel occupations involve working with brick and stone. As well as building and maintaining houses, you might work on large commercial projects. You may also be involved in converting or extending existing buildings.

Bricklayers and stonemasons

Bricklayers build and maintain many kinds of structures, including the external and internal walls of houses and commercial buildings. They also work with various materials and use specialist tools to spread and joint **mortar** and cut bricks or blocks to the correct size.

below: *Bricklaying can be tiring work, but it can be satisfying to see your building take shape.*

Some bricklayers specialize in stonemasonry work. Stonemasons prepare and cut stone and bricks to produce architectural features such as window frames and archways. These jobs can be very creative. Stonemasons often restore historic buildings and monuments, so an interest in history may be useful.

For these jobs you will need to be physically fit and enjoy working in a team. You should not mind working in all weathers or high above the ground, or doing repetitive work. Accuracy is crucial.

Getting in to bricklaying

You will need a Maths GCSE or S-grade (Standard grade) for carrying out calculations and measurements. It will also be helpful to take English, Design and Technology, and maybe Art. There are **City and Guilds**, **Edexcel**, and **Construction Industry Training Board** (CITB) courses in bricklaying available at Further Education (FE) colleges. To train as a stonemason you could take a CITB Construction Award in Stonemasonry or a City and Guilds stonemasonry course.

A good way to enter the industry is by training as an **apprentice**, starting at age 16–19. You will train on the job, with day or **block release** at a local college for your studies.

CASE STUDY

Sam is a trainee stonemason.

I'm 18 years old and have recently left school. I started work as an apprentice stonemason 3 months ago. I didn't have any experience in the trade but I did study Art and Design at school, which is recommended by the CITB for this trade. Maths is useful, too, because masonry is really all about lines and measurements.

The company I work for supplies stone for various jobs, for example, stone for fireplaces. At the yard, we load blocks of quarried stone on to the saw to cut to size. Once the stone is cut, most of it needs to be cut to the right size and shape.

In this job you have to concentrate hard all day long. If you lose focus, you may take the corner off the piece you're working on.

below: *Stonemasons work on precious historic buildings.*

Working with wood

Think of all the wood in your own home: floorboards, skirting boards, window frames, and doors. Carpenters and joiners make wooden structures and fittings for homes and other kinds of buildings. You could be building storage shelves in a warehouse or doing formwork – making wooden structures to support setting concrete during the construction of a bridge. If you decide to be a bench joiner, you will work mostly in a workshop preparing doors, windows, staircases, and furniture.

You might be interested in becoming a shopfitter, who plans and fits the interiors of all kinds of shop, from little corner shops to huge department stores. You will need some creative flair for this trade. This is a job at the finishing end of construction, so you will need to work accurately and be a bit of a perfectionist to satisfy your clients. After all, you will have influence over the look and feel of the shop and will help to make it a place where people want to spend some time – and their money!

below: *Accurate calculations are essential for making sure the wood fits perfectly!*

Site workers will need to work in all weathers and all conditions and sometimes in cramped conditions. Bench joiners work in workshops, which get very dusty. Everyone who works with wood will have to wear safety equipment, such as goggles and ear defenders, at least some of the time.

Get ahead!

As a carpenter, joiner, or shopfitter you can progress to technician level and construction management. Check out the possible career structure for shopfitters at www.shopfitters.org. Alternatively, you could move into a specialized area of work such as building restoration or furniture making.

Why work with wood?

Working with wood can be very satisfying as well as being a creative job. Many people will appreciate your work. There are also plenty of opportunities for self-employment. If you gain experience in shopfitting, for example, you will be in a great position to set up your own business. Carpentry, joinery, and shopfitting are skilled **crafts** in which you will learn to use lots of specialist tools.

The skills you need

If you are thinking about these trades, you will need to have excellent hand–eye coordination, a head for figures, and be able to work accurately. It is important to be able to follow technical drawings correctly. You will find it useful to achieve GCSEs or S-grades in Maths, English, and Design and Technology. Maths is particularly useful for measuring and calculations.

Most people go into these jobs through an **apprenticeship**. You will probably have to go through a selection test to get a place. You could also attend a course at an FE college to study for an Edexcel, City and Guilds, or CITB qualification in carpentry and/or joinery.

Are you a bright spark?

Electricians are involved in construction – they install, inspect, and test wiring systems. Currently, there is a shortage of electricians, so if you can get wired up to the necessary skills, you will have good career prospects. Many organizations and individuals employ electricians.

Working as an electrician

If you would like to be an electrician, it is good to be flexible, as the industry needs people who can work overtime in the evenings and at weekends. You might even need to work overnight to minimize disruption to the inhabitants or workers in a building. You will need to be physically fit and prepared to work high up or underground. If you're working on a new building, you may be working in an uncomfortable environment – it could be cold, damp, dusty, and dirty.

above: *Working as an electrician often means working in a challenging environment.*

CASE STUDY

Catherine is on a 4-year electrical apprenticeship, learning to be an electrician. She left school age 16 with nine good GCSEs, including her favourite subject, Electronics.

I am the only female apprentice on my course. I've been put off in the past by employers and tradesmen who did not want to work with a woman, but I've been very determined and worked really hard. I was the first in my group to complete my apprenticeship at NVQ Level 2. Now employers ask for me to be a part of their team. I work mainly on electrical installation and maintenance. We go into houses to repair sockets and lighting, install storage heaters, and often carry out complete rewires.

Apprenticeship

The usual route to become an electrician is through an apprenticeship, which lasts 3 or 4 years and gives you practical, work-based experience. There are no formal entry requirements if you want to start an apprenticeship, although GCSEs grades A–C or S-grades 1–3 in English, Maths, Design and Technology, and Science subjects may be requested. Applicants must also pass an **aptitude test** to check if they are suitable for training and also take a colour vision test. Generally, you need to be practical and able to use power tools. It is essential to be safety conscious and to keep up to date with changes in technology.

Get ahead!

As an electrician you can get into specialist jobs such as panel building. Panel builders put together electrical and electronic control panels to manage office systems such as heating and ventilation. Specialist electricians keep the traffic lights working on highways. They have to find and repair faults quickly.

right: *Good colour vision is important to electricians, so they can tell wires apart.*

Chapter 2

The great outdoors

Outdoor construction jobs include roofing, **scaffolding** and demolition, and operating plant. If you are fit and strong and have a head for heights, there could be something here for you!

Roofing

With the windy climate in the UK, there is plenty of work making, repairing, and **renovating** roofs.

Roofers work with various materials, including tiles, slate, felt, and mastic asphalt (a waterproof material often used on flat roofs). Some roofers specialize in one kind of material. Felt roofers apply felt in several layers to form a waterproof covering. Roof slaters and tilers place individual tiles or slates on to a timber framework.

To be a roofer, you will obviously need to be happy working outdoors. It can be cold and windy in winter. In summer, a roof can get extremely hot as heat is reflected from the surface. Working at height is dangerous, so you will have to be conscious of health and safety issues. The standards for installation and building regulations are always changing, so you will need to keep up to date with your field.

You will work a normal working week compared to many other construction workers. You may need to work on weekends but you will not have to work night shifts up on the roof!

CLIMBING SKILLS

Many roofers who are skilled at climbing and maintaining their balance become successful rock climbers in their spare time.

Getting into roofing

◎ It is useful to obtain GCSEs/S-grades (4–7) in Maths, English, and Design and Technology so you can cope with the calculations, measurements, and theory involved in the job.

◎ Most people enter through an apprenticeship. You will train on the job while studying at college for **National Vocational Qualifications** (NVQs) and **Scottish Vocational Qualifications** (SVQs) in built-up roofing or roof slating and tiling.

◎ You can train through the Institute of Roofing.

◎ Another option is to take a CITB Intermediate/Advanced Construction Award at Further Education (FE) college.

Get up the career ladder!

You might get to work on an exciting project such as fitting the roof to a new sports stadium. There are also some impressive renovation jobs also available. It is possible to work your way up to become a supervisor or manager or to set up your own roofing company.

STAYING SAFE

Falls from height are the biggest cause of death in the workplace. In 2004–2005, 28 people in the UK died this way. The Work at Height Regulations of 2005 state that where people work at height, they should use equipment to prevent falls. If they cannot eliminate the risk of a fall, they should use equipment to minimize the distance and consequences of a fall if it happens. Check out the website of the National Federation of Roofing Contractors (www.nfrc.co.uk) for details.

right: *The first part of every roofer's job is to make sure the working conditions are safe.*

Scaffolding and demolition

Scaffolders put up scaffolding so that new buildings can be constructed and maintenance and cleaning work can be carried out on existing buildings. As a scaffolder, you might be putting up scaffolding around a house or a commercial block, or even around a historical monument so that it can be restored. Scaffolders also erect structures, such as stages and spectator stands, for outdoor events.

Putting up scaffolding is a skilled job. The scaffolding is made from metal tubes, fittings, and wooden or metal platforms, which are put together so that workers can get to the parts of the building they are constructing.

Knock-out jobs

You may not believe it, but demolition work is also a skilled job. It is not just a case of blowing buildings up and watching them tumble down! As a demolition operative, you may be dismantling anything from a chimney to an old power station. Sometimes you will be working with specialist drills and cutting equipment. Other times you will need to operate heavy machinery or use explosives.

Get ahead!

From scaffolding or demolition, you could progress to supervisory roles, estimating, or construction management. If you have **Computer-Aided Design** (CAD) skills, you could go into project design or management.

above: *Good, safe scaffolding is essential before any work can be done on the outside of a high building.*

Holly is a demolition operative.

In this job it is essential to know about health and safety issues as you may come across hazardous materials, such as lead and asbestos, that can harm human health. Part of my job is to remove these materials and dispose of them safely.

To bring down a large structure, explosives are often used. The end result is spectacular! No two jobs are the same. I've had to climb up to heights of over a hundred metres before to place charges.

above: *Working in demolition can be an exciting job!*

Getting into scaffolding and demolition

To be a scaffolder or demolition operative, you will need to be happy working outdoors in all weathers and at height. You will need to be strong for carrying and lifting heavy equipment. It is a tough job physically and you will be on the go all day long. Demolition operatives also need to have good **manual skills** for operating equipment.

At school, it will help if you have GCSE passes/S-grades in Maths, English, and Design and Technology. If you're thinking about being a demolition operative, Science subjects are also relevant.

Training and progression

◎ There is special training for scaffolders through the Construction Industry Scaffolder's Record Scheme (CISRS) and you could also take relevant National Vocational Qualifications (NVQs) or Scottish Vocational Qualifications (SVQs.)

◎ You need to be over 18 to train as a demolition operative. You will have extensive safety training, learn first aid, and will work towards your Certificate of Competence for Demolition Operation. You can also undertake special training in using explosives in demolition.

Plant

Do you like the idea of driving heavy vehicles – or fixing them? These monsters often go wrong, so if you're technically minded, being a plant mechanic could be the job for you. You will have to be prepared to work away from home on site and the conditions can be cold and dirty. Awareness of health and safety issues is crucial.

left: *Plant vehicles can be enormous like this one.*

Becoming a mechanic or plant operator

◎ To be a mechanic, you usually need four GCSEs (grades A–C) or S-grades (1–3), including Maths, Design and Technology, and Science.

◎ To be a plant operator, knowledge of vehicle engineering and GCSEs/S-grades in Maths, English, and Design and Technology are helpful, but not essential. You will need to be over 18 to start your training.

Most people enter these jobs through an apprenticeship. Major companies offer 4-year apprenticeship schemes, which include supervised work experience and block or **day release** at college, leading to NVQ/SVQs in Plant Operations or Plant Maintenance (Construction). When you start your training, you will probably be tested on your technical and mechanical understanding.

Myrtle is a plant operative. Here he describes how he got into the job.

I drive diggers and dumpers and put pipes in the ground. I've been doing the job for 7 or 8 years.

I left school at 17 and worked on a farm for a while. Then I started working as a labourer on construction sites. I had no previous experience, but I learnt from older people on site. I did all sorts of different jobs. I was always fascinated by large machinery. I used to have a go at driving the large machines in my lunch hour and fancied being a plant operative. In the end I got the job I wanted. It doesn't bother me working outdoors in the wind and rain. I love the job because every day is different.

If you want to do this kind of work, I'd recommend going straight into the job and training while you're working. You can't learn to operate machinery in the classroom – you need hands-on experience. However, you need to be patient. At first, you will get the worst jobs on site and the pay is low. Lots of people leave after 3 or 4 months. But if you stick with it, after a year or 18 months you will earn better money and get more interesting tasks to do.

Make sure you work for your NVQs. Your company should offer you NVQ training – I'm working towards NVQ Levels 3 and 4 at the moment. Having the qualifications really helps you, especially if you want to switch jobs.

below: *It takes great skill to repair complex and expensive plant machinery.*

Chapter 3

An inside job

Many jobs in the construction industry involve working indoors, for example, plumbing, plastering, and painting and decorating. These jobs suit people with excellent manual skills who are good planners and have a head for figures. You will work mainly indoors but will have to cope with the cold, dirty, and damp conditions in uncompleted buildings.

Plumbing

Wherever you have lived, the chances are that your family has had to call out a plumber at some point. Plumbers install and maintain water supplies and sanitation and waste disposals systems. If your washing machine floods, your toilet leaks, or your drains are blocked, a plumber can fix the problem. Plumbers also install and maintain boilers and central heating systems.

Plumbers work in all kinds of properties, from homes to commercial and industrial premises. They can work independently or as part of a building team on big projects. There is a big demand for skilled plumbers, both in the UK and abroad.

Skills required for plumbing

◎ Plumbers have to be flexible as they are often needed in an emergency. You could be on call 24 hours, 7 days a week. It is also common to work overtime.
◎ You will need to be able to follow plans carefully and work accurately and tidily.
◎ It is important to be physically fit. Bear in mind you could have to work at heights and sometimes in cramped, uncomfortable spaces.

CASE STUDY

Paul is a gas plumber.

Doing pipework can be fiddly. At the bottom of a boiler, you need to connect the gas pipe, a vent pipe, a hot water pipe, a cold water pipe, and pipes to all the radiators. They all go in different directions so it can get confusing and there's a lot of thinking involved.

above: *Plumbers may have to work in unpleasant conditions.*

Training to become a plumber

To get into plumbing, you generally need four GCSEs (grades A–D) or S-grades (1–4) in subjects such as Maths, English, Science, Design and Technology, or suitable alternatives. It will help to take up an apprenticeship to enter the industry.

You will learn theory at college and practical skills on the job with your employer. You will need to study for technical certificates to prove that you understand plumbing theory and work for National Vocational Qualifications (NVQs) through your practical experience.

The main fields that plumbers can go into include:

◎ heating
◎ ventilation
◎ refrigeration
◎ electrical and air-conditioning industries
◎ gas fitting.

Some plumbers work in ship or marine plumbing, the chemical industry, or the gas supply industry.

ENERGY EFFICIENCY

In 2005 new strict controls were brought in to make sure that domestic boilers are energy efficient. These regulations are part of the drive to encourage people to save energy. If you install boilers for domestic heating, you will need to get training whenever new regulations are brought in.

Get ahead!

Find out about the main fields that plumbers can go into. Start with the Learn Direct website (www.learndirect-advice.co.uk).

Plastering

No decorating job will ever be right unless a plasterer first creates a good base underneath. Plasterers apply coats of plaster to walls, floors, and ceilings. There are different kinds of work:

◎ Solid plastering gives an even surface on walls and ceilings.
◎ Fibrous plastering is used to make patterns for ornamental plastering.
◎ Drylining is for making wall linings and partitions.

Plasterers work for construction companies, either as employees or **subcontractors**.

What skills do I need?

To do this job you will need to be good at working with specialist tools and not afraid of heights. You may have to work on scaffolding, platforms, and ladders. You will need good coordination and be able to work quickly – plaster dries fast. If you are going to do decorative work then it would help to have some artistic skill.

below: *Plastering work always requires a steady hand.*

WORKING CONDITIONS

Plastering work is normally indoors but the conditions can be cold and damp, and it is a messy job. As for all construction jobs, you may need to travel or spend time away from home.

Getting the skills you need

At school, you should work for GCSEs or S-grades in Maths, English, Craft, and Design and Technology. These qualifications will help you with the calculations, measurements, and theory. Good numeracy skills are particularly important for calculating surface areas and volumes of materials required.

Most people become plasterers through an apprenticeship. There are also City and Guilds and Construction Industry Training Board (CITB) plastering courses available at Further Education (FE) colleges.

Get ahead!

Ornamental plasterwork is in fashion! If you get into this area of plasterwork, you will make items such as **ceiling roses**, **cornices**, **coving**, and arches. You will often need to follow drawings by an **architect** or interior designer, or photos of old plasterwork, and use special moulds or casts to create the patterns. You will mostly work in a workshop but may sometimes make on-site visits.

CASE STUDY

Daniel is a trainee plasterer.

I left school 2 and a half years ago. I started out as a labourer, tried my hand at plastering, and liked it. I'm learning on the job with an experienced plasterer. I don't go to college as there are no courses near by.

At first I found it frustrating because I couldn't get it right, but I watched and learned, and after a few months I realized I'd got it. I enjoy plastering because you can just get on with the work on your own. We are doing a big renovation job at the moment and I plastered a couple of large walls by myself.

I like the security of working for a company. If we are on an outside job and it is raining, my boss will find me something else to do, so I'll still get paid.

Painting and decorating

A painting and decorating job might sound easy – just putting a lick of paint on the walls! This is, however, just a small part of the job. As a painter and decorator, you could be redecorating the inside and outside of people's homes, but you might also be doing heavy-duty work painting bridges or ships. The job includes stripping and cleaning the surfaces to be painted to ensure they are smooth. You then seal them with a primer (a first coating of paint) and paint undercoats and topcoats of paint. Sometimes, you will put up wallpaper.

below: *A painter puts the finishing touches to the name on a ship's stern.*

Working conditions

As a painter and decorator, you can work on your own, as part of a team in a construction company, or for a specialist painting and decorating firm. You will generally work a normal working week, but you may need to work overtime to ensure a job is finished on time.

Get ahead!

If you're artistic, you could go into special effects, for example, using stencils to produce patterns and pictures. You could also move into a related career such as interior design.

Be prepared for hours of working on your feet and a lot of bending down. There may be both indoor and outdoor work, and you may need to work at height. The tools you will use include brushes, rollers, and spraying equipment. Some paints give off fumes, which can be unpleasant and bad for your health, so sometimes you will have to wear a protective mask. This is often a demanding job, but when you have finished, it can be rewarding to see the newly painted structure gleaming and fresh.

above: *As a painter and decorator, you could use your creativity to produce some amazing designs.*

Is painting and decorating for you?

As well as being creative, you will need to be well organized and able to work accurately. Good colour vision is required for mixing paints and a flair for design is also helpful. If you are working for individual customers, it is important to be able to get on well with them and understand their needs.

Get ahead!

If you want to progress to technician or supervisory level, you may need four GCSEs (grades A–C) or S-grades (1–3), A-levels or Highers, or a vocational college qualification. Alternatively, you could set up your own painting and decorating business.

Getting into painting and decorating

There are no fixed entry requirements but some employers may expect you to have some GCSEs or S-grades in subjects such as Maths, English, and Design and Technology, or equivalent vocational qualifications such as an Edexcel Introductory Certificate/**Diploma** in Construction, which contains options in Painting and Decorating. Alternatively, you can go to FE college and take a City and Guilds or CITB course in Painting and Decorating.

A common route into the job is through an apprenticeship. At college, you will work towards NVQs or SVQs in Decorative Occupations (Construction) Levels 2 and 3.

Chapter 4

Get technical

If you are technically minded, this area of the construction industry could appeal to you. Technicians support all aspects of construction work.

Computer-Aided Design

There are various jobs using Computer-Aided Design (CAD). Software is used to generate drawings to prepare for a construction job. As a civil engineering technician, for example, you would use CAD to produce drawings and plans for all kinds of structures, such as roads, bridges, or large buildings. You would then visit the site to ensure the work is going according to plan.

What skills do I need?

To be a CAD operative you will be into computers and have an interest in art and design. It is useful to know about construction methods. Good communication skills are essential as you will be working with different groups of people, such as site teams, materials suppliers, and engineers.

You will usually need GCSEs (grades A–C) or S-grades (1–3) in Maths, Science, and Design and Technology. These will be useful for the calculations, measurements, and theory.

below: *Computer-Aided Design can really bring construction plans to life.*

Buyers and sellers

Every construction project needs someone to ensure the correct number of bricks is delivered to the right place on the right day – and that the price is also right. This is the buyer's job. Buyers need to be well organized and good at dealing with people. There are no particular entry requirements but it is useful if you have already trained in another area of construction. A common way in is through an apprenticeship.

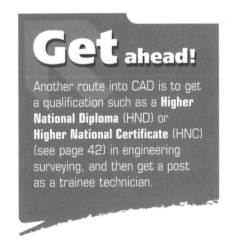

Get ahead!

Another route into CAD is to get a qualification such as a **Higher National Diploma** (HND) or **Higher National Certificate** (HNC) (see page 42) in engineering surveying, and then get a post as a trainee technician.

On the other side are the salespeople, who sell goods and services to clients on behalf of a construction company. For this job you need to be confident and outgoing, persuasive, and good at negotiating prices. There is no specific route to get into the job; many people transfer to sales from other parts of the industry.

Estimators

A large construction project can easily go over **budget** and take far longer than expected to complete. As an estimator, you work out the cost of the project from the plans and the buyer's list and estimate how long the job will take – no easy task! You will work for a building company or **subcontractor** and liaise with clients to keep them informed of progress.

TECHNICAL JOBS

Other technical jobs include the site technician, who helps organize the general running and safety of the site, and the plant technician who organizes the use of machinery.

There is no specific entry requirement, but it is helpful to have already worked in the industry. GCSEs (grades A–C) or S-grades (1–3) in Maths, Science, and Design and Technology are useful. Apprenticeships are available for trainees.

Chapter 5

The management

All construction jobs need to be well planned and organized – and that's where management comes in. There are various levels of management, including the project manager, construction manager, and company manager.

Project manager

The project manager is in charge of a construction project. He or she has overall responsibility for the planning and management of the job, including the budget and schedule. Project managers are also responsible for health and safety matters. They have to be aware of all activities that are going on and make sure that they are carried out safely and to the agreed method.

below: *The project manager must make sure that everyone is aware of all the health and safety issues surrounding the construction project.*

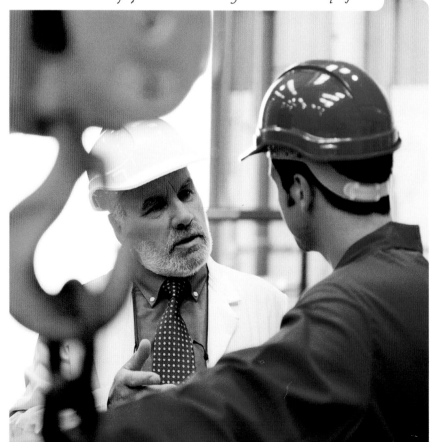

Construction and facilities manager

◎ The construction manager is in charge of the building site and makes regular safety inspections, dealing with any problems that arise.

◎ A facilities manager comes in once the structure is complete. The job involves keeping everything running smoothly and making repairs or improvements to the building as necessary.

Relevant degrees

To be a project manager or a construction manager, you will need a degree in Building Studies, Building Management, or an equivalent.

CASE STUDY

Andrew is a project manager for a civil engineering company that builds roads and bridges.

I've been a project manager for 5 years. I started out in civil engineering 15 years ago, setting out on sites and then moving into project management. I managed small projects at first then moved on to bigger and bigger projects. In my last job I was responsible for a budget of over £50 million to construct 10 kilometres of motorway in Ireland.

I have to gather together the people, machines, subcontractors, and specialists to build a team. I then manage them to make sure they deliver the project to the satisfaction of the customer and that my employer makes a profit.

*I recruit graduates and **mentor** them as they train to be **chartered** civil engineers. I look for reasonable academic qualifications, but more importantly, people who are practical, logical, and don't mind tramping around in mud most days.*

I'd advise students to focus on the career they want and tailor their school studies to lead to that career. If you go to university, choose your course carefully and make sure it is a degree that is recognized by employers.

Talk to the bosses

If you are thinking about going into construction, what skills and attributes will impress your potential employers? Firstly, motivation is a must. If you are not keen on the job, it will show. This is why it is so important to consider carefully which area of work to enter.

The ability to communicate clearly is vital. If you are not sure what you are doing or you are unhappy about an issue at work, you need to be able to express yourself to your boss. This will help improve your own learning and performance in the job. Linked to this are teamwork and negotiating skills. Even if you dream of working solo, you will need to learn alongside others to achieve the skills to do this. A vast range of people from different backgrounds and with different opinions may work together on a construction project. Bosses appreciate it if you can get on well with your co-workers.

IT skills are useful in various areas of the industry, especially in technical roles. Maths is also essential, especially calculation.

CASE STUDY

David is the manager of a small construction company.

I've been running my own construction company for 4 years. I've got six employees and four subcontractors who work for me pretty much permanently.

As we're a small company, we don't have the resources to take part in apprenticeship schemes. But I do take on school leavers from time to time. The main thing I look for is basic common sense. I like the young people to ask questions the whole time – that's how they'll learn. At first, they need to be willing to do any task at all. It is true that they'll get the horrible jobs to start with, but if they stick with it, the work will become more interesting. Another big issue for me is timekeeping. Many of the young people I've taken on haven't seen how important it is to turn up on time.

My advice to young people is to consider carefully what you want to do when you leave school. So many people start out in construction and soon realize it's not for them. Also, you have to be patient. You're not going to earn top money right from the start. You have to work your way up.

As to how to start, I think the best way to learn and get qualified is to become an apprentice with a large company.

Transferable skills

You may have already gained skills from holiday or part-time jobs. You have probably developed communication and problem-solving skills and have learnt how important timekeeping is when working with customers and other employees.

Get ahead!

Many of the big construction companies have websites that offer helpful information on career paths, so check them out. Some of the bigger companies are listed on page 38.

below: *Being able to work well in a team will help jobs on site run more smoothly.*

Chapter 6

Work experience

When you are in Year 10 or 11, your school will organize for you to do work experience – usually for 2 weeks in England and Wales, and for 1 week in Scotland.

The world of work

The purpose of work experience is to give you an idea of what it is like in the world of work. Many students feel more motivated in class afterwards because they can see the relevance of what they are learning in school to a job they might do. Often they feel more mature after spending time in an adult environment and being treated as one of the workers rather than as a school student.

Finding placements

On average, about 50 per cent of all placements are found by a local Education Business Partnership, an agency outside the school. The remaining 50 per cent of placements are found by the school or by the students and their families themselves. You should get a choice of placements, but you will not always get your first choice. Before you start, a health and safety check will be carried out to make sure the workplace is a safe environment for you to work in. You will do preparation work at school, most of which is devoted to health and safety. Check your route to the workplace so you can turn up on time, and make sure you know how to dress appropriately for the job.

Get ahead!

Check out the National Council for Work Experience site at www.work-experience.org. It includes links to other websites that help students to find placements and contains students' stories about their work experience.

On placement, the most common activity for students is to help a co-worker to do their job, while many do an actual job themselves. Each day you will complete a diary and log book, and some students will also interview people in the workplace. Usually, your teacher will visit at some point to see how you're getting on.

above: *Work experience is a really valuable way of understanding more about the world of work.*

Types of placements

◎ Short placement – usually carried out for a short block during the school year, typically 2 weeks in the summer term.

◎ Extended placement – lots of choices for extended placements are available and it can take the form of 1 or 2 days each week over a period of 1 or 2 years.

Feedback

When you return to class, there will be a debriefing so you can talk about your experiences, and you will be assessed on your log book or diary. It is useful to summarize your experience. The following checklist may help.

WORK EXPERIENCE CHECKLIST

◎ List the good points about the placement.
◎ What training did you receive?
◎ Did you have enough help to carry out the work?
◎ Were you able to use your **initiative**?
◎ Did you come across any conflict and how did you resolve it?
◎ Were there any bad things about the experience? If so, what did you learn from them?
◎ Has your work experience helped you decide what you would like to do for a job?

The bigger the better?

You may do your work experience in a large or a small company. The advantage of working for a large company is that you will work with a variety of people and see how various trades come together to work on a project. In large companies it is also common to take on apprentices, so there is a structure for incorporating learners.

Get ahead!

Find out about local construction companies that offer work experience. Go to the website for the Construction Industry Training Board (www.citb-constructionskills.co.uk) to access information about your regional office.

below: *There are many different jobs to choose from on large construction sites like this one.*

Small is beautiful?

About 90 per cent of construction firms have ten or fewer employees. These companies don't carry out as huge a range of work as large companies. However, if you do work experience for a small company, you will get a good idea of the overall running of the business as well as some insight into the trade you are interested in.

right: *In a small team you may have to do several different jobs.*

CASE STUDY

Daniel is in Year 10 at secondary school in Scotland. He did work experience with Steven, a self-employed laminate floor layer. (Laminate flooring is made from artificial materials to look like wood.) Daniel got involved in all aspects of Steven's work.

On Monday, we laid laminated kitchen tiles. We measured the kitchen floor and then we put down the underlay. After lunch, Steven showed me how to cut the tiles. He did the first few rows and then I had a shot at it. We worked together, but Steven did the tricky angles. Once we'd fitted the floor, we cut and nailed the beading (edge pieces) to the wall and cleared up our mess.

On Tuesday, we used a different type of laminate that was much easier to use. All we had to do was line it up and click it into position. I got to use the nail gun to fit the beading. The next day, we had to get up really early to buy supplies for the job. On Thursday, we drove to the job in the van. The house was huge – as big as a palace! We laid hard laminate in the bedroom. We had to slide it into position and then click. It only took us 2 and a half hours to lay the floor. On Friday, we had a small hall to cut and fit, which was pretty easy to do.

I really enjoyed my work experience with Steven and he was glad to have my help.

Chapter 7

A foot in the door

So, how do you get into the construction industry? You can either go straight into a job, work and study part-time, or study for qualifications before seeking a job. Alternatively, you can do a degree and enter the industry later on.

On the job at 16

Even if you cannot wait to leave school and get a job, make sure you leave with some qualifications to help you get into the trade you have chosen. It is helpful to get several GCSEs/S-grades, especially in Maths, English, Design and Technology, and Science. In some schools in England and Wales you can take a Foundation Certificate in building craft occupations.

To get into a craft trade at 16 years of age, you will need to have a good basic education, including some GCSEs/S-grades. You will learn skills on the job and find out about construction materials and methods. For a technical trade, you will need four GCSEs/S-grades. In both craft and technical occupations, it is possible to gain qualifications while you work.

LARGE COMPANIES

Some of the large construction companies in the UK are listed below. This list may help you think about the area you would like to work in. Check out each company's website for more details.

◎ Alfred McAlpine – public sector construction such as schools, hospitals, airports, and roads
◎ AMEC – oil and gas facilities, transport systems, schools, hospitals
◎ Balfour Beatty – roads, rail, utility systems
◎ Carillion – roads, rail, hospitals
◎ Costain – civil engineering such as bridges, Channel Tunnel
◎ John Laing – roads, rail, and privately financed public sector projects such as roads, railways, hospitals, and schools
◎ Kier – civil engineering, house building, mining
◎ Mowlem – infrastructure such as roads, rail, water and utilities, and building projects
◎ Taylor Woodrow – house building.

Learn while you earn

Apprenticeships (**Modern Apprenticeships** in Scotland) are a highly recommended way for young people aged 16–24 years to enter the construction industry. You work and earn a wage while following a structured training programme, for an average of 3 years.

The Construction Apprenticeship is for young people aged 16 and over – their employer sponsors them while they complete the apprenticeship. You will gain qualifications as you train. Craft trainees gain a Construction Award, while technical students gain a National Certificate. You can learn more about the qualifications available by checking out the Construction Skills website at www.constructionskills.net.

Get ahead!

Whilst you work, you can also study towards National Vocational Qualifications (NVQs) or Scottish Vocational Qualifications (SVQs). (See page 40 for more details about these qualifications.)

above: *These modern apprentices have got the chance to work on an aircraft jet engine.*

Qualifications explained

At age 16, you can study full-time or part-time at Further Education (FE) college. There are various qualifications available and they are constantly changing. This can be quite confusing! Research the options carefully to see what will suit you best. You can work towards:

◎ Construction Awards
◎ National Award/Certificate and National Diploma
◎ National Vocational Qualifications (NVQs)/Scottish Vocational Qualifications (SVQs)
◎ Vocational GCSEs and A-levels.

Get ahead!

It is worth checking the Ofsted report for the course you plan to take to see if it has been rated as satisfactory.

Construction Awards (England and Wales)

These qualifications are available at three levels (Foundation, Intermediate, and Advanced) for students on apprenticeships, and are based on college work alone. You may have the opportunity to take the Foundation level at school.

National Award/Certificate

These courses lead to a technical qualification. They are usually taken by people who are training on the job, although you can study full-time. Students generally spend 1 day a week at college and work the rest of the week. The National Diploma is a similar technical course, which people generally study full-time.

NVQs and SVQs

NVQs and SVQs are work-related qualifications that are available for almost all occupations. They demonstrate your overall competence and knowledge of the craft.

NVQs and SVQs can be taken by full-time employees or by part-timers who are also attending college. You achieve them through training and assessment of your practical skills. You also collect evidence to prove you have the skills and knowledge to meet the standard for your NVQ Level. There are five levels of NVQs/SVQs. During your first 3 years of training, you will probably work towards Levels 1–3.

above: *Practical work is a very important part of construction-related courses.*

GCSEs and A-levels in vocational subjects

These introduce you to a sector of work and prepare you for further vocational study or a job. A GCSE in a vocational subject is equivalent to two GCSEs. From 2007 a GCSE in Construction and the Built Environment will be available.

Alternatively, you could take non-vocational A-levels or Highers, giving you the option to enter a trade at 18 or to continue your studies further.

Get ahead!

From 2008 14–19 year olds will be able to take a Specialised Diploma in Construction and the Built Environment while they are still at school.

CARD SCHEMES

By 2010 everyone working in the construction industry will need to prove they are competent to do the job. Card schemes have been introduced to provide a standard system to assess competence. To get your card, you will need to have an NVQ/SVQ at the right level for your job and pass a health and safety test. There is no formal exam – you simply collect evidence to prove you know what you are doing, and this evidence is checked.

above: *A qualification in a construction-related subject can be a good start to a career in construction.*

Technical and university courses

If you are over 18 you can go to FE college and study for a Higher National Certificate (HNC) or Higher National Diploma (HND). These are technical courses in a range of areas of construction and the built environment. To get onto a course, you will need a National Certificate, A-levels, or Highers (see pages 40–41). An HNC course lasts 1 year full-time and 2 years part-time, while an HND takes 2 years full-time and 3 to 4 years part-time. This means that you can study part-time and work as well.

Another option is to take a **Foundation degree** at FE college, which is a suitable vocational qualification if you want to move into a technical job rather than a craft. It takes 2 years full-time and 3 years part-time.

Alternatively, you can take a university degree. You may be able to get sponsorship with an employer to do a sandwich course, which includes periods of employment. The employer will offer you some money while you study, and once you have graduated you will get a permanent job with the company.

CASE STUDY

Steve mixed study and work experience.

I'm a graduate site engineer working on a road-building project in England. Throughout my studies, I always did work experience. First I studied for a certificate in civil engineering, which took 2 years. After I finished, I did a summer job working for a contractor laying telecommunications ducts. Then I enrolled on a diploma course. Following that, I spent the summer working as an engineer, helping to design water mains. When I went to university, I continued the job at weekends and in the summer holidays.

*I did really well in my first year at Queen's University, Belfast, and was allowed to transfer to a **Masters** course in civil engineering. In my final year, a team of three of us produced a dissertation (an extended essay) on bridge design. The university entered it into a national competition and we won first place! I know this helped me get a job later. Meanwhile, during my final 2 years at university, I worked for a company that designed **retaining walls** and learnt to use electronic engineering software. I completed my Masters with first-class Honours and was offered a job with my current employer.*

My advice to students is to take time out for work experience to make sure you are suited to the field you're interested in studying. Speak to people in the job to get a real picture of what it involves. It may be extremely satisfying and worthy, but may also mean working long, unsociable hours for a small financial reward. Best to know this from the start!

Chapter 8

Climbing the career ladder

Many skilled professionals are needed to plan and organize a building project before the craftspeople and technicians can get down to the job. For these top construction jobs, you usually need to have a degree. You can do a degree before you find a job or work for a few years before taking professional qualifications.

Join the professionals

Here are some of the professional jobs you could do:

◎ A land surveyor checks the features of the landscape where the construction is to take place – it is important to know you will be building on solid ground! A combination of a degree and on-the-job experience are necessary to qualify for this profession.

◎ A civil engineer is responsible for transforming the plans into reality, which involves liaising with suppliers, setting out, dealing with any design changes, and coordinating the various trades on the job. You need a Higher National Diploma (HND) or a degree to train in this profession.

◎ An architect designs the building in great detail, making drawings by hand and using Computer-Aided Design (CAD). This calls for great creativity and a talent for design, and you need a degree in architecture to begin your training.

left: *It takes many years to qualify as an architect because it is a highly skilled job.*

Get ahead!

Check out Planning and Management jobs at www.bconstructive.co.uk/careers/. Click on Choose profession.

- Another vital member of the organizing team is the construction manager, who coordinates the site workers and deals with problems that arise. A degree is also essential for this job, but you can study for it part-time while working as a technician or craftsperson.
- At the head of the team is the project manager, who has overall responsibility for completion of the project (see pages 30–31). To get into this job, it is common to obtain a degree first, but it is also possible to work as a technician and take a degree later on.

Town planners

Some people work on a bigger scale than individual construction projects. If you are interested in a fulfilling job with a huge impact on people's lives, town planning could be an option. Town planners supervise the development of a town or region. They have to try to balance the needs of the population, the economy, transport systems, and the environment. You will need to liaise with other professionals and present your plans to the public – and deal with any criticism and conflict over planned developments.

below: *Site managers check the architect's plans are being followed correctly.*

Career planning

It can take many years to fully qualify in some professional jobs:

◎ Architecture – 7 years' training: a 3-year degree, 1 year in an architectural office, a 2-year diploma, and 1 year's work experience.

◎ Civil engineering – a degree followed by professional training, for example, a National Vocational Qualification (NVQ) / Scottish Vocational Qualification (SVQ). You then need to pass a professional review. You have to be at least 25 years old to register as a qualified civil engineer.

◎ Town planning – a degree followed by a postgraduate certificate (4 years full-time or 5 years part-time), then 2 years' professional experience to become a member of the Royal Town Planning Institute.

CASE STUDY

Manjeet is a trainee surveyor.

After having children I decided to start a new career and I'm in my third and final year of a degree in surveying. I've been interested in construction since I was a child.

I decided to study to be a surveyor because there is a huge demand out there. There are also few women surveyors, and companies are often keen to take on a woman to adjust the gender balance a little.

I'm doing work experience 1 day a week with a local company. I love going on site. The builders seem to have a great respect for surveyors. When I'm out on the job, everything I've learnt in the classroom starts to make sense.

Last week I had to go up a really high ladder over a busy road to access a building I was surveying. Luckily I'm not scared of heights! It makes me realize that safety issues are crucial in this line of work. Sometimes people don't follow all the safety guidelines though – and they should!

I also enjoy the design side of the job – doing technical drawings for new buildings and renovations.

When I've finished my degree, the company I'm working for will take me on full-time. Then I need to do 2 years' further work experience before I can become a chartered surveyor. This is definitely worthwhile. You have to be chartered if you want to set up your own practice. It also means you are better qualified and you can earn a higher salary.

In the future I'd like to get a job with the local council because this will be relatively secure and the hours are more flexible than with a private company.

above: *To become a surveyor you will need a degree and professional training.*

Get qualified later

Some people work in a craft or technical job and decide later to take professional qualifications. You could be an experienced site technician, for example, and study part-time for a degree with sponsorship from your employer. Once you have successfully completed your course, your boss may offer you a job as a construction manager – with a nice pay rise!

Other people have worked in an entirely different field and want a career change. It is possible to gain new skills and qualifications through work experience and a course at college or university that will allow you to find a professional job.

Stay ahead of the game – keep learning!

Whatever area of construction you go into and at whatever level, you will always need to keep learning. It is important to keep up to date with changes in your field and general construction issues, such as changes in building regulations and new measures to protect the environment.

There are National Occupational Standards for each trade, which describe what an individual needs to know and be able to do to carry out a particular job. They help you to assess what stage you have reached in your training and plan your career development.

Each craft and profession has its own national organization that promotes training and the maintenance of high standards among members. The Institute of Carpenters, for example, offers various craft awards for carpenters and joiners looking to enhance their range of skills and qualifications.

Get ahead!

You may be able to get specialist training through your industry's national organization. Alternatively, your company may run a training scheme or you can arrange to take further NVQs through your local college. Various organizations offer qualifications for the construction industry, including the Construction Industry Training Board (CITB), City and Guilds, and Edexcel.

NATIONAL SKILLS ACADEMY

The government is planning to open a network of twelve National Skills Academies by 2008, one of which will focus on construction. The aim of the National Skills Academy for Construction is to help reduce the shortage of skilled workers in construction. It will consist of a network of on-site training centres based at major construction sites around the country, which will be supported by mobile training centres. Training will be offered according to the needs of the project in hand. Keep an eye on the progress of this initiative when you are planning where to train.

Olympic opportunities

The construction of the Olympic Park in East London for the 2012 Olympic Games will be the biggest single construction project in Europe. There will be a main stadium, an aquatic centre, and an Olympic village. After the Games, the athletics and swimming centres will remain open for the training of future sportsmen and women, while the village will provide much-needed housing. Thousands of construction workers and technicians will be required, not only in London, but also at many other venues around the country where events will be held. This will be an opportunity to work on a project with many challenges and huge long-term significance. Could this be the start of your career in construction?

TRAINING FOR CONSTRUCTION

At school up to age 16	◎ GCSEs/S-grades
	◎ Foundation Construction Award
	◎ Foundation Certificate in building craft occupations
	◎ Specialised Diploma
Get a job at 16 years+	◎ Get a craft or technical job
	◎ Apprenticeship
	◎ Take NVQ/SVQs while you work
Study at age 16	◎ Construction Award
	◎ National Award/Certificate
	◎ National Diploma
	◎ A-levels/Highers
Study at age 18	◎ Higher National Certificate
	◎ Higher National Diploma
	◎ Foundation Degree
	◎ Degree
Professional qualifications	◎ Company training
	◎ Further NVQs
	◎ Postgraduate diploma
	◎ Qualification through a professional organization

Jobs in construction

Architect

Architectural technician

Architectural technologist

Bench joiner

Bricklayer

Building control surveyor

Building engineer

Building services engineer

Building surveyor

Built-up felt roofer

Buyer

CAD operative

Carpenter and joiner

Ceiling fixer

Civil engineer

Construction manager

Demolition operative

Dry liner

Electrician

Estimator

Facilities manager

Floor layer

Form worker

General construction operative

General practice surveyor

Geomatics surveyor

Geospatial engineering surveyor

Geospatial modeller

Geotechnical engineer

Glazier

Health and safety officer

Hydrographic surveyor

Joiner

Land surveyor

Landscape architect

Lead sheeter

Liquid waterproofing systems operative

Logistics manager

Managing director

Mastic asphalter

Painter and decorator

Partitioner

Planner

Plant mechanic

Plant operator

Plant salesperson

Plant technician

Plasterer

Plumber

Project manager

Quantity surveyor

Renderer

Roof and shelter cladder

Roof slater and tiler

Roofing technician

Salesperson

Scaffolder

Shopfitter

Single-ply roofer

Site engineer

Site inspector

Site technician

Steel erector

Steeplejack

Stonemason

Structural engineer

Supervisor

Town planner

Wall and floor tiler

Wood machinist

Rough annual earnings for jobs described in this book

- **Bricklayer** – starting salary: £14,500 to £16,500; qualified: £17,000 to £22,000
- **Buyer** – assistant: £16,000; senior: £26,000
- **CAD operative** – £15,000 to £40,000
- **Carpenter/joiner** – starting salary: £13,500 to £16,000; qualified: £17,000 to £22,500
- **Construction manager** – starting salary: £20,500 to £25,000; experienced managers: £26,000 to £35,000
- **Demolition operative** – trainee: up to £12,500; qualified: £13,000 to £18,000
- **Electrician** – newly-qualified: £16,500 to £19,000; experienced: £20,000 to £25,000
- **Estimator** – assistant: £17,000; senior: £28,000
- **Painter and decorator** – starting salary: £13,500 to £15,500; qualified: £16,000 to £20,000
- **Plant operative** – trainee: up to £13,000; qualified: £14,500 to £18,000
- **Plasterer** – starting salary: £14,000 to £17,000; qualified: £17,500 to £22,000
- **Plumber** – newly qualified: £16,500 to £20,500; experienced: £21,000 to £26,000
- **Project manager** – at least £31,000
- **Roofer** – starting salary: £13,500 to £16,000; qualified: £16,500 to £21,000
- **Scaffolder** – trainee: up to £13,000; qualified: £16,000 to £23,000
- **Stonemason** – starting salary: £14,000 to £16,500; experienced: £17,000 to £21,000

Note: Senior craftspeople with long experience will earn more than the figures shown.

Please note that qualifications and courses are subject to change.

Publications

◎ Apel, Melanie Ann. *Careers in the Building and Construction Trades* (Rosen Publishing Group, 2005)

◎ Green, R. *Discovering Careers for Your Future* (Facts on File Inc., 2001)

◎ O'Connor, Rachel. *Construction Worker* (Children's Press, 2004)

◎ Pasternak, Ceel. *Cool Careers for Girls in Construction* (Impact Publications, 2000)

◎ *Working in Construction* (Connexions, 2004); also available as a PDF from www.connexions-direct.com

Careers websites

◎ City and Guilds (www.city-and-guilds.co.uk)
   – This website tells you all about City and Guilds qualifications.

◎ Connexions Direct (www.connexions-direct.com)
   – You will find advice for young people here, including learning and careers. Includes link to the Jobs4U careers database.

◎ Learndirect (www.learndirect-advice.co.uk) and Learndirect Scotland (www.learndirectscotland.com/)
   – Go to the job profiles for details of many jobs in the construction industry and courses and qualifications.

◎ Modern Apprenticeships, Scotland (www.scottish-enterprise.com/modernapprenticeships)
   – Check out the case studies of people already training.

◎ Need2Know: Learning (www.need2know.co.uk/learning)
   – Look here for information about studying and qualifications.

◎ Qualifications and Curriculum Authority (www.qca.org.uk/14-19)
   – Go to "Qualifications" and click on "Main Qualification Groups" to find out about NVQs.

◎ Scottish Vocational Qualifications (www.sqa.org.uk)
   – Find out all the latest qualifications information for Scotland here.

◎ The National Council for Work Experience (www.work-experience.org/)
   – Go to "Students and Graduates" to search for placements.

Get ahead in Construction!

◎ Bconstructive (www.bconstructive.co.uk)
  – This site tells you all about how to get into the construction industry.

◎ Careers in Construction (www.careersinconstruction.com)
  – This is a leading recruitment site with daily news and CV tips.

◎ Construction Industry Training Board (CITB)
  (http://www.citb-constructionskills.co.uk/)
  – Look here for training and qualification information.

◎ Union of Construction, Allied Trades and Technicians (UCATT)
  (www.ucatt.org.uk)
  – This is the UK's only specialist construction workers union.

Useful organizations

◎ Chartered Institute of Building (CIOB)
  (http://www.ciob.org.uk/ciob)
  Englemere
  Kings Ride
  Ascot, Berkshire, SL5 7TB

◎ Institution of Civil Engineering Surveyors (ICES)
  (http://www.ices.org.uk/mac1000.htm)
  Dominion House
  Sibson Road
  Sale, Cheshire, M33 7PP

◎ The Institution of Engineering and Technology
  (http://www.theiet.org/)
  Savoy Place
  London, WC2R 0BL

◎ Royal Institute of British Architects
  (http://www.riba.org/go/RIBA/Home.html)
  66 Portland Place
  London, W1B 1AD

◎ The Royal Town Planning Institute
  (http://www.rtpi.org.uk/)
  41 Botolph Lane
  London, EC3R 8DL

apprentice person who is on a training scheme to become qualified in a trade

apprenticeship training scheme that allows you to work for money, learn, and become qualified at the same time

aptitude test test to evaluate how people perform on tasks or react to different situations

architect person who designs buildings

block release period of time, usually several weeks, during which an employer allows you to be away from work so you can go to college

budget money that is available for a job and a plan of how it will be spent

ceiling rose circular fitting on the ceiling for attaching a light

charges quantity of explosive to be detonated

chartered someone who has reached the required standard to practise in his or her profession – for example, a chartered engineer has satisfied the requirements of the Institute of Civil Engineers

City and Guilds leading provider of vocational qualifications in the UK, assessing practical skills that are of use in the workplace

civil engineering design and construction of public works such as roads and bridges

Computer-Aided Design (CAD) programme that creates computer-generated drawings to prepare the information required for a construction job

Construction Industry Training Board (CITB) organization that helps to recruit, train, and provide qualifications for workers in construction

cornice decorative band of wood used to hide curtain fixtures

coving curved moulding that connects walls to the ceiling

craft job in which you need good manual and often artistic skills

day release way of working where your employer allows you to go to college for a day a week

diploma vocational qualification usually taken after secondary school to provide you with employment skills. There are also postgraduate diplomas (diplomas completed once you have a degree).

Edexcel leading provider of vocational qualifications in the UK, similar to City and Guilds qualifications (see City and Guilds)

Foundation degree vocational degree, recommended if you want to go into a technical, engineering, or supervisory job rather than a craft

foundations layer of bricks, concrete, or other material that forms the solid underground base of a building

Higher National Certificate (HNC) technical qualification that you can take after a National Certificate or after A-levels/Highers

Higher National Diploma (HND) technical qualification that you progress to from an HNC (see HNC). Usually takes 2 years to achieve.

initiative doing something without being prompted by someone else

manual skills skills that involve using the hands or physical strength

Masters second or further degree

mentor experienced person who trains and counsels new employees or students

Modern Apprenticeship Scottish apprenticeship, lasts for 4 years

mortar mixture of sand, water, lime, and cement used in building to hold bricks and stone together

National Vocational Qualification (NVQ) in England and Wales, a work-related, competence-based qualification that shows you have the knowledge and skills to do a job effectively. NVQs represent national standards that are recognized by employers throughout the UK.

plant heavy machines, such as cranes, used on building sites

professional to do with a job that requires specialist training

renovation restoring or improving an existing building

retaining wall wall to prevent the movement of rock, soil, or water down a slope

setting out transfer of information from a designer's drawings to the situation on the construction site

scaffolding temporary structure for workers to stand on while they are working on the outside of a building

Scottish Vocational Qualification (SVQ) in Scotland, a work-related, competence based qualification that shows you have the knowledge and skills to do a job effectively. SVQs represent national standards that are recognized by employers throughout the UK.

subcontractor firm with experts in a particular area, which is hired by a construction company to do certain tasks

sustainable buildings that are built and can be used with a minimum of resources. They create little waste and will not harm the health of the people who use them, now or in the future.

trade job or occupation. Also used in the same way as "craft".

trades union organization of workers that aims to protect workers' interests and improve their working conditions

Union of Construction, Allied Trades and Technicians (UCATT) specialist construction workers' union in the UK and Ireland

ventilation system that allows fresh air to enter and move around a building

Index

Titles in the *How to get ahead in* series include:

Hardback 978 1 4062 0442 1

Hardback 978 1 4062 0443 8

Hardback 978 1 4062 0440 7

Hardback 978 1 4062 0441 4

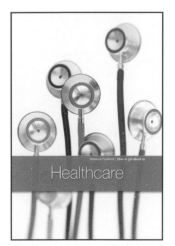

Hardback 978 1 4062 0444 5

Other titles available:

Armed and Civilian Forces	Hardback 978 1 4062 0450 6
Finance	Hardback 978 1 4062 0448 3
IT and Administration	Hardback 978 1 4062 0449 0
Leisure and Tourism	Hardback 978 1 4062 0447 6
Retail	Hardback 978 1 4062 0446 9

Find out about the other titles in this series on our website at www.raintreepublishers.co.uk